TERROR ON THE COAST

THE WRECK OF THE SCHOONER *CODSEEKER*

92 93 94 95 96 97 98 8 7 6 5 4 3 2

Produced as part of the Nova Scotia Museum Program
of the Department of Education, Province of Nova Scotia

MINISTER: The Hon. Guy J. Le Blanc
DEPUTY MINISTER: Armand F. Pinard

Co-Published by Nimbus Publishing Limited
and the Nova Scotia Museum

A product of the Nova Scotia Government Co-Publishing Program

DESIGN, TYPOGRAPHIC FORMATTING & ILLUSTRATION
Ivan Murphy

LASER IMAGESETTING
Braemar Imaging Services, Halifax, N.S.

FILM & PRINTING
McCurdy Printing & Typesetting Ltd. Halifax, N.S.

CANADIAN CATALOGUING IN PUBLICATION DATA
Easton, Alan 1902—
Terror on the Coast (Peeper)
Co-Published by the Nova Scotia Museum
ISBN 1-55109-025-2

1. Codseeker (Ship)
2. Shipwrecks – Nova Scotia – History
i Nova Scotia Museum. ii Title. iii Series.

G530.C63K37 1992   910.4'5   C92-098727-3

TERROR ON THE COAST
THE WRECK OF THE SCHOONER *CODSEEKER*

By Alan Easton

Illustrated by Ivan Murphy

Co-published by
NIMBUS PUBLISHING LIMITED
and
THE NOVA SCOTIA MUSEUM
Halifax, Nova Scotia
1992

DEDICATION

*For the descendants
of those who suffered
in this tragedy*

ACKNOWLEDGEMENTS

N WRITING THIS EPIC OF THE SEA, I AM INDEBTED TO Marion Robertson of Shelburne, a Nova Scotian historian, for having provided me with such essential records as could be gathered after a hundred years, and for persuading me to put them into narrative form.

I have used my own words to clarify for the general reader the behaviour of vessels under sail and the handling of boats. Also some of the descriptive passages of the sea are mine. These aspects are commonplace for fishermen, thus they were seldom recited in documentary statements. If I have added anything else it has been to present what obviously took place where such minor realities were left unwritten in the records.

I really first heard of the story some years ago in Ottawa from then Dominion Archivist, Wilfred Smith, who was a great nephew of James Edwin Smith, one of the protagonists; but I did not think seriously of it then as it seemed too remote. Marion Robertson eventually changed my mind.

Thanks also to:

Niels Jannasch
Marven Moore
David Flemming

Nova Scotia Museum
members of the
Publications Committee

Barbara R. Robertson,
Editor

Alan Easton
Montgomery Center
Vermont
1992

TERROR ON THE COAST

CHAPTER ONE

THEY TRIED TO ROW BACK TO THE STRICKEN SCHOONER but they had drifted too far while bailing out the dory. They had managed to launch it, but the seas kept breaking inboard threatening to swamp them again. The intense darkness and the flying spray made it difficult to search the sea, and moreover, only the side of the schooner's black hull was above water.

Captain Philip Brown, of the fishing schooner *Codseeker*, and his two men at the oars reluctantly set a course to leeward, turned their small craft away from the wind and from those left aboard the capsized vessel. The dory was inclined to yaw, and they had all they could do to keep it from broaching to in the easterly gale, one of the last of that spring of 1877. The light mast and sail had disappeared when the other dories had been swept away, but in any case, the sail would have been too flimsy for such a wind. The Cape Sable Light, sentinel of the southwest extremity of the ruggedly indented coast of Nova Scotia, guided Brown towards the shore. They had only eight miles to go if he could beach the boat in the right place. But he needed daylight. Brown knew it couldn't be done in the dark. It was now midnight, so the dory had to be kept before the heavy sea for some seven hours.

The three men were already soaked, and had it not been for the vigour with which the crewmen rowed while Captain Brown worked furiously at the bailing, the cold that penetrated their sodden clothing would have numbed them to incapacity. Doryman John Smith had lost his sou'wester, which he had been using to bail out the boat, the bucket having been washed away, and his matted head glinted as the revolving light of Cape Sable

Thwart:
The wooden seat
in a small boat

Transom:
The flat stern
or back end
of a dory

came around. Rain squalls added to his discomfort and would have disheartened a less hardy soul. Though accustomed to oars, none of them would have chosen to be trapped in a gale and forced to pull a fourteen-foot dory in such a sea.

The Captain changed places with the seamen periodically to modify their toil; he could rely on either to keep watch on the course. The cook, Nathaniel Knowles, on the after-thwart, let go his oars, moved into a crouching position in the stern and bailed, while Brown fell onto the vacated thwart and picked up the rhythm of the rowing. Knowles looked up often to check the bearing of the flashing light and give a directional word. After a long time, Smith took over the bailing, although it was awkward for Knowles to climb forward to relieve the bowman and for Smith to make his way aft to lean against the transom.

The night seemed to last forever as the strain continued. The wind raised a higher sea. The difference was plainly recognizable to the rowers facing the overtaking waves that curved higher and reached out to catch them, their rolling tops white against the darkness. Yet the dory with her high sides and seaworthy narrow stern withstood its onslaught. The wind, persistent in direction but occasionally faulty in strength, gave the men a little respite at times. These lulls, brief moments when smaller, crisscrossing waves fell in between the larger ones, allowed the Captain's mind to dart back to his schooner.

Why had she so suddenly fallen over? She was under shortened sail, and the wind was not too hard for her. She was on shoal ground where the seas would be short and steep, but that was not enough. He could not fully understand her behaviour; it was not quite that of any other schooner he had sailed on in his twenty-six years at sea. She seemed to have no stiffness in her, her centre of buoyancy was too high. Yet it was hard for him to believe that he had lost his fine new vessel by sailing her down. He thought of the men he had left on deck. Were they washed off? He could not dwell on such speculations now. The dory mounted another precipice, thrashed and twisted.

At last, a faint dawn came up; they should be near the shore. Too much water was sloshing around in the boat. Brown told

Knowles to join him in bailing, while Smith handled the oars alone; the dory must not be waterlogged for what was to come.

The light on Cape Sable had just become hidden, indicating that the land at the point had intervened, but Brown could still see the loom of it in the sky occasionally. Thus he knew how close he was. He would like to have made the Hawk Channel and gotten around to the other side of the island to beach the boat in the lee of the land, but as daylight grew, he could see nothing but misty sea at short range.

After a while the rain stopped and visibility increased under the overcast sky. And there stretched a dim, dark ridge. The shore! Brown saw, as they rose out of a trough, a low white mist on the surface of the water before the shore. The men at the oars glanced round. The surf! It was a frightening sight and they were glad to turn their gaze away. They thought they could hear it even above the sound of the wind.

Captain Brown had a fair idea of where he was. He had been born and raised at Bear Point on the mainland, just across from Cape Sable Island, so he knew the island's rocky shores and few sandy beaches, stony sometimes after storms. He had left home when he was twelve, like other lads, to fish on the Banks. He could make out The Hawk a couple of miles to the south but knew he could not reach it; the dory could not withstand the gale beam-on nor keep off the lee shore. He must stand straight on.

Knowles and Smith seemed to row more slowly as the pitiless surf, now heard clearly, raced in a full quarter-mile, perhaps to a beach, perhaps to a ledge of rock. Brown muttered to himself, "Thank heaven it's close to high water." The dory swept forward, first lifting high on the riven backs of the breakers, the spume tearing from their crests, then plunging down into deep, white-streaked, black hollows.

Weary, yet desperately alert, each man acted independently, judging when to ease his oars, when to pull harder. They rose and rode over an outer curling wave, as they had ridden over others in the night, but this one had greater driving power. The oarsmen, with their backs to the inner surf, watched the approaching breakers; the captain's gestures guided them on their course.

The surf forging towards the shore roared like a hundred cataracts. Brown's heart beat faster. Could they survive what lay beyond? The roar grew louder, and the spray often obliterated his view of that dark outline, the land. And worse, he thought he saw rock-born pillars of water, their flying plumes flattened by the wind. Though sturdy, the dory felt smaller. It hovered in the furrowed rollers, assumed precipitous angles, ascended the oncoming heights stern first, was forced to feebly plane, was racked by the crashing tops.

With their feet firm and oars secure between the thole pins, the two dorymen pulled and eased according to the pressure of the sea. And so they rushed in with the high combers, the colliding, crossing waves, the forever-shrieking wind, the roar of the surf, the blinding spray. Reaching shallower water in shelving ground, the boat leapt violently and almost pitched over. It was like a twig in a tide rip. But by an instinct born in fishermen, they held on.

Suddenly they grounded. The jolt unseated the rowers, and the crouching captain sprawled forward. The dory swung abreast the sea and threw them out, They staggered in the shifting sand and stone beneath their feet, and knees bent, bodies leaning forward against the tow of the receding wash, they fell on the beach. By the grace of God, it was a beach.

The bitter wind beat against their saturated clothing, accentuating the chill of their bodies. Each with effort pulled himself up, took a few unbalanced steps, feet squelching in leather seaboots, then climbed the ridge beyond the loose sand and reached the coarse grass above.

The house they saw was no more than three hundred yards away, just around the head of South Side Inlet. They leaned back against the onshore wind; it helped them along on their cramped and unsteady legs. Banging on the door, Brown threw it open and was met by Delick Nickerson, known to them all.

"My Lord! Where you from?" Nickerson exclaimed.

Philip Brown looked intently at him with eyes still screwed

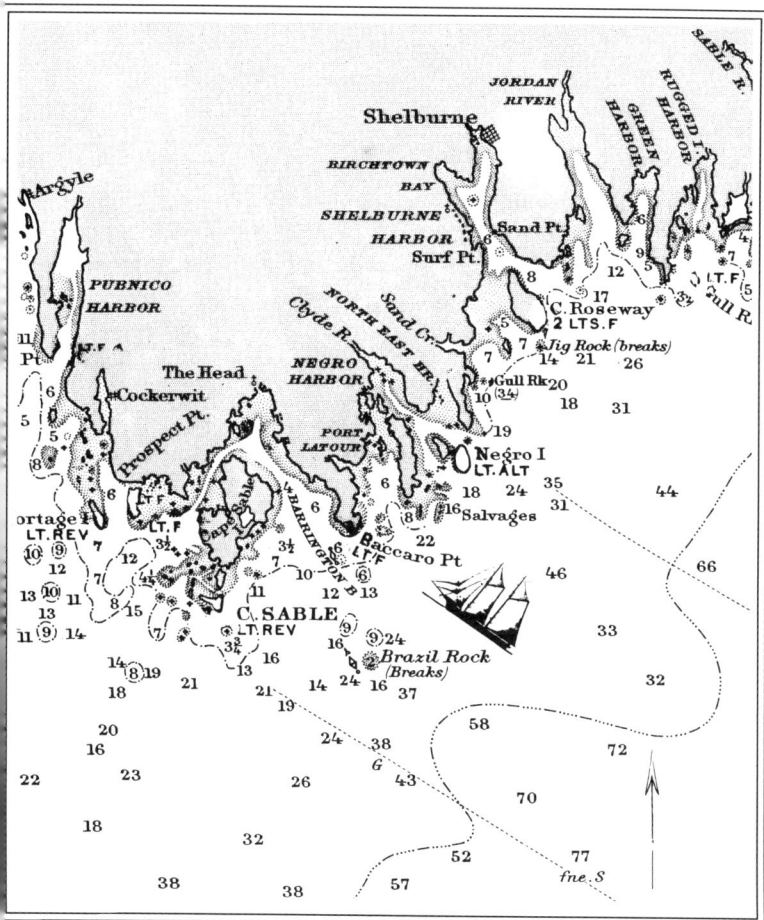

The province of Nova Scotia, *above*, and *left*, a nautical chart of the area around Cape Sable, with the approximate position of the Codseeker when she capsized

up as though peering through cutting spray. He told him in a few hoarse words.

"Codseeker, she's laid down. Got to get a vessel to try to save the men we've left ... if they be still aboard."

"You come through that?" Nickerson shouted incredulously, jerking his thumb towards the sea.

"Yeah," Brown replied. "Somehow."

The man, who had harboured other survivors of shipwrecks, helped them strip off before the stove, threw blankets and old coats over them, poured black rum into mugs and thrust them into shaking hands. His wife put a pot of oatmeal back on the range.

"Where be the Codseeker to?" Nickerson asked.

"Off Baccaro. Full gale."

Nickerson frowned, looking at the men who periodically fell to shivering. He addressed Brown.

"I got enough clothes for you, Phil; maybe you'll have to wear your wet boots. Then we'll get over to Clark's Harbour if you be up to it."

Brown and his benefactor left within the hour.

During the two-mile trudge along the track, a shortcut over to Clark's Harbour on the other side of the peninsula, Brown had anxious thoughts again. Had any other members of his crew withstood the powerful buffeting of the sea on the capsized hull? He had to find out. He knew that he had not abandoned them without warrant. By leaving them and making that implacable night passage there was perhaps a chance, a slender chance. His safe arrival might yet be timely. But he felt himself too spent to join in the search. He had to stop to take off his tall seaboots and scrape more sand out of them with his fingers; Nickerson, recognizing the weariness of his companion, did not speak.

MAIDEN VOYAGE

CHAPTER TWO

THE TWO-MASTED SCHOONER *CODSEEKER* HAD BROUGHT a catch of mackerel into Halifax the previous Friday, which Captain Philip Brown had sold at a reasonable price. On the morning of May 8 he cast off and sailed up the coast to the small port of Prospect where he intended to buy bait, before going straight out to the Grand Banks. But when the schooner reached Prospect in the afternoon he found that bait was scarce, so he decided to run on to his home port of Barrington where he reckoned there was plenty.

The schooner was new. She had been launched and fitted out the month before in Thomas Coffin and Company's yard at Port Clyde near the head of Cape Negro Harbour and was now making her maiden voyage. The Coffins were builders of many splendid schooners and square-rigged ships, which were to be seen thrashing across the oceans of the world. The *Codseeker* was constructed for Reuben Stoddart who for many years had been the company's master builder. Of forty-two tons, she was a sharp, deep vessel, fifty-eight feet long with a beam of eighteen and a half feet; she carried the standard rig with the usual gaff topsail when under full sail. The amount of ballast a vessel should have was always a question in the mind of a builder, and perhaps Coffin had considered that the *Codseeker* did not need as much as was generally placed in the hull because of her grip of the water.

At dawn on May 9 the captain weighed anchor and with his crew of twelve men passed out through the rocky mouth of Prospect Harbour and stood into a moderate sea to make an offing. He set a course of west-sou'west before a fresh easterly breeze. As the dull afternoon advanced, the wind increased and the schooner, being light, sped on, her fore and main booms well out, her new sails full. The crew occasionally sighted land broad to starboard as the hard outline of a promontory became etched clearly in the rain-threatening atmosphere.

At dusk the sky became more heavily overcast and nimbus clouds darkened the low grey ceiling. The evening was more like March than May though the lingering light lasted longer.

As the dismal day faded Brown saw Cape Roseway Light abeam at about eight miles distant. The wind strengthened to half a gale, which was not unusual with the coming of night, and the schooner was driving hard when the captain, shouting above the sound of the sea and the whine of the wind in the rigging, ordered the mainsail lowered. He caught the rise and drift of responsive cries. The mast hoops clattered as they slid down, and with wet work at the outer end of the boom the stiff sail was furled.

Soon afterwards he hauled in towards the land gybing the foresail so that the easterly gale took her on the starboard quarter. Brown figured that he was off Blanche Island, probably to the southeast of it, when the lookoutman, who had to leave the foc's'lehead to make himself heard, reported breakers ahead. The master kept the schooner going. The man at the wheel heard him say, mainly to himself, "Reflection of Cape Sable Light on the wave tops, that's all," He had seen the flash intermittently, but he understood the apprehension of the young seaman watching the bows. The older experienced fisherman at the wheel murmured, "Hope he be right." He was.

At about 10:30—Brown guessed the time since he did not want to open his oilskin coat to reach inside for his watch—the light at Baccaro Point punctured the horizon fitfully, and he set his course directly for it by sight rather than by the compass, which was swinging erratically. The darkness was intense, yet now and then the phosphorescence of the sea illuminated the form of the breaking waves as they came up under the schooner's quarter, lifting and rolling her to conform to their steep contours.

They hauled the jib halfway down. Brown thought she rode more quietly now, but he soon changed his mind. To his senses the wind's tune had altered; it was louder, a strong gale was blowing, though not yet a full gale, and it was inevitably driving the seas

Gale:
A strong wind blowing at a velocity between 35 and 60 nautical miles an hour. Within this range of wind velocities, mariners distinguish between a moderate gale, a fresh gale, a strong gale and a whole gale

To Reef:
To reduce the area of sail spread to the wind by tying up the lower part of the sail

higher. But he knew he was on the Shoal of the Rock where he would expect a shorter and steeper run of sea. He was not much disturbed; no need to reef the foresail. And he could see Baccaro Light at the entrance to Barrington Bay around which he would gain a comfortable lee. Four miles would do it.

But the *Codseeker* was rolling heavily, almost unnaturally, weaving too, with the rise and fall of the stern. But she was light, her hold was empty, which partly accounted for her tenderness. Her masts made a short swing to starboard then a long sweep to leeward; she was lethargic in righting.

Perhaps it was a squall, perhaps it was that one wave was higher than the others. She lifted her weather quarter, pitched and rolled down, her speed arrested by the drag of her bulwarks ploughing under water. She hung, hesitant—so did the hearts of the fishermen. Then she continued her downward roll, gradually careening over until she lay flat on her beam-ends. It was eleven o'clock. The condition was borne in on all hands instantly. Half the vessel's deck was submerged, her sweeping forward charge gone; she lay inert, dead, wallowing in the storm with half her bottom exposed to wind instead of water.

Captain Brown (whose full statement was made to the notary public in Barrington four days later) leapt to the cabin combing and so to the rail. He clung there for a while, incredulous. Then he crawled back to the transom where several men had gathered to try to launch the large boat carried at the stern, but she was hanging vertically in the davits. Undaunted, they cut the weather tackles, the uppermost, but could not reach the falls at the other end, which lay six or eight feet under water. They gave up that means of escape.

The hands aft clung to the high side of the derelict while the captain worked his way amidships to the starboard nest of dories between the foremast and mainmast. Two dories had gone, one was left floating but entangled. Two men (the cook and a young fisherman) were trying to release it. Together with the captain they dislodged it and, getting into it, managed by pushing and pulling to manœuvre it clear of the spars and rigging. The foresail was a further hindrance lying sodden in the water with its boom thrashing free. As soon as they got through the maze they had to bail out the water. Lightened, the dory drifted faster than the schooner and was soon far down wind. They took to the oars.

There were eight men on deck besides the master when the *Codseeker* capsized, and four below, one man in the cabin and three in the foc's'le, counting James Edwin Smith who had just gone below. He had been forward when they had half-lowered the jib, and when that was done he had gone aft in case the captain had wanted the foresail reefed.

He had been thirsty, so after watching the motion of the vessel he seized the opportunity as she rolled up to go down for a drink. When descending the companion ladder into the foc's'le she lurched sharply to leeward and he saw his ditty box, containing such treasures as he had, shoot out of his berth. He rescued them as she recovered and then made his way to the cook's water bucket. But just as he was dipping the tin mug into it while holding on to a stanchion with the other hand, the deck became very steep, then gradually steeper. To his dismay the schooner was falling over. The oil lamp swinging from the deckhead went out, and Smith slid to the ship's side. He could not see the companionway, but he knew where it was and strove to reach it, groping his way over lockers already under water. He got his foot on the bottom step though it was perpendicular and found the handhold. But the cascade of water coming it through the opening at the ladder top was already so powerful that his hand was wrenched from its grip, and Smith was swept back into the dark cavern. He did not feel the stunning encounter his head made with some hard object; he was knocked senseless.

Six men were left on deck when the dory got away: Jesse Smith, Jeremiah Nickerson, William H. Goodwin, Zebe Hunt, William E.

Kenney and Crowell Nickerson. They had all done as the instinct of preservation directed—they never let go whatever they could grasp until they caught another piece of standing gear.

The schooner was lying stretched out with her keel towards the wind. Because of her rounded hull and her drift she did not present a rock-like resistance to the waves but rather a contour, like a sluice over which at intervals the seas swept clean as a green tide. There was nowhere to go for protection. The deck, above water from the centreline to the bulwark, resembling a swaying wooden wall. Along the top of this wall each man finally secured himself to the bulwarks or to the now horizontal shrouds with such rope as he could lay hold of at the time. Though the schooner seemed to swallow tons of water as she rose and fell it was disgorged as fast as it went in; she would stay afloat. The gale increased in ferocity as the hours wore on.

The wet inert men were pounded at times against the life-preserving bulwarks or twisted in the rigging as waves fell on them and threatened the capacity of their lungs while they waited for the water to pass over them. In the lulls they felt the soreness of their chafing sodden clothes beneath the lashings. The cold was constant; only youth and hardihood kept their blood circulating.

The lines they had uncoiled from the belaying pins in their early need and desperation were new and stiff and on this account tended to work loose at the knots; nor could they be tightened as old rope could. It was probably this fatigue accompanied by numbness that released Crowell Nickerson from the bonds that held him. Without an audible cry he was suddenly washed out of the shrouds.

Dawn came gradually, bleak and desolate, the gray scudding clouds low over the racing billows and the derelict still drifting with her masts to leeward as when she had been hove down. It was in the faintness of the daylight that the survivors of the night discerned Nickerson's body, a bundle of tattered clothing, lying in the belly of the undulating foresail apparently held there by tangled cordage.

The voice of the wind, the constantly repeated surge of the seas lashing them, bombarded the ears and senses of the five men left—until there came the silence of immersion. They had been thus exposed for nine hours. Clothes had been ripped: Goodwin's oilskin was in two strips and slapped his bare head in the gusts until he contrived to tear it off with a free hand. Both of Jesse Smith's seaboots had been sucked off long since, the others too had lost one or both.

Full daylight revealed the devastating turmoil of the ocean in the narrow visible circle of the spray-filled mist and the clear impression of their drowned companion dipping and rising a few yards before them. In a rare lull, Kenney's plaintive voice was heard patiently singing, evidently in dedication to Nickerson. His words swelled and faded:

"Jesus, lover of my soul, let me to Thy bosom fly."

He got no further but started again as though he had forgotten the rest. The others feebly joined him while the wind seemed to hold back.

"While the nearer waters roll, while the tempest still is high." There the hymn was swallowed up with thunder and slashing rain.

The morning hours dragged only a little less slowly than they had in the night, desperately slowly. Their hopes, when their minds were released from the pains of their flesh and perishing cold, had almost fled. They knew they could last only a little longer. How could they be found when no one knew what had happened?

SCHOONER MATCHLESS RESPONDS

CHAPTER THREE

WHEN DELICK NICKERSON AND PHILIP BROWN REACHED the wharf at Clark's Harbour they saw no fewer than thirty schooners tugging at their anchors riding out the storm. The surface of the water was more white than black, overlaid with shifting patches of spindrift. Captain Brown paid no attention to it, though he did not ignore the meaning of such a fleet of sheltering vessels. He was unsteady as the two approached the wharf.

A group of six or eight men stood in the shelter of a fish shed. They turned their gaze from the moored vessels and vicious water to the arrivals. Brown did not hesitate.

"*Codseeker's* adrift on her beam-ends," he announced over the sound of the gale in a stronger voice than his companion would have credited him with.

"*Codseeker!*" They knew Philip Brown was her master. "Where to?" They gathered around him.

"Beyond Cape Sable by now probably. Anyone ready to go out to find her?"

An incredulous one spoke, "New boat! How?"

"Just went over."

"Where be the crew?"

"Most still aboard if God's with 'em."

There were exclamations and quick glances at the water and at Brown.

"How did you get away?"

"He came in a dory," exclaimed Nickerson, annoyed.

"Dory! Good God!"

The terse response sank in and, to one in particular, more deeply than the rest.

"You think they could have lived in that in a capsized vessel out off Sable?" asked Captain Job Crowell pointing towards the harbour.

"Don't know," Brown answered. "That's what I want to find out."

Crowell asked several further questions and on receiving appealing replies looked once more at the storm-swept roadstead protected by the land though it was. After a pause he spoke again.

"My crew went home when I brought the *Matchless* in last evening. I'll round 'em to and if they be agreeable I'll go, but ..." He did not finish. The others stared at him.

"Can't go out in that there," one said nodding his head towards the harbour, his hands deep in his pockets. "No master would try to."

Several boys were on the wharf hanging round listening. Crowell made use of them sending them off to notify his crew naming each man—though the boys knew who manned every local vessel.

"Tell 'em to come to the wharf quick as they can; we may go out on a rescue job."

The news of the *Oudooher's* plight spread through the village with the boys' progress. More people gathered on the waterfront as most of the crew of the *Matchless* hurried down. The position was briefly drawn by Philip Brown, and the proposal to sail put before the men by Captain Crowell, though he knew how they would answer.

The volunteers were Joseph Williams, Stillman Crowell, Reuben Penny, Benjamin Newell, Jedah Crowell, George Phillips, Nathaniel Crowell, Peleg Nickerson and Captain Henry Brown, brother of Captain Philip Brown.

It was about ten o'clock when the villagers watched a seine boat being pulled with streaming oar blades between the anchored schooners towards one of the few whose master would have chosen to go out. Embarking her crew, already wet, the seine boat was warped astern to be towed.

The two-masted schooner *Matchless* had been built in Essex

Seine Boat:
A transom-sterned or
double-ended rowboat,
approximately
twenty-eight feet long,
normally used for
carrying a long
seine net

Massachusetts, several years previously and was owned by Captain Job Crowell and his father Eleazer, a Clark's Harbour merchant. Job Crowell had sailed her as a trader on the New England and Nova Scotia coasts and sometimes as a fisherman. Her home port was Clark's Harbour where she was regarded as a sturdy, well-founded vessel—the inhabitants knew the worth of every vessel registered in the port. Captain Crowell was twenty-four and had learned the ways of schooners since he was twelve like most Cape Islanders.

With a number of other schooners he had sought refuge the day before in the late afternoon, after delivering a catch of mackerel to a Maine port. Crowell had wasted no time making for his home port when he saw his barometer falling steeply and the ominous appearance of the sky.

That foul morning of May 10 Captain Crowell weighed his two anchors, set his jib and threaded his way between the ranks of moored vessels making for the open water. As he reached it he ordered the foresail hoisted, double reefed. Thus he sped on a course to the south'ard under the protection of the land, though mostly no more than sand dunes, rolling heavily and intermittently plunging to the fore rail.

He did not see Green Island but caught sight of the rip over Cook Ledge. After four miles they felt the devastating force of the easterly, and Crowell knew he had cleared Cape Sable. He swung to a course of west by south and ran before it, the shriek of the wind in the rigging changing to a lower pitch. But they were fully aware of their loss of shelter and the swiftness with which wave succeeded wave with vicious power.

Where was Job Crowell to look for the *Codseeker*? He had a clear picture of her position when she had capsized the night before, as described by Philip Brown, and had calculated her drift westward in the gale and tidal streams. She must have passed the Cape some hours before. The course he had just set was the most likely. But in the murk the range of sight was extremely short. To look at all was almost useless. He could hardly think about searching; the behaviour of his vessel under the violent pressure of the sea demanded almost all his attention. Was he foolhardy?

He knew he probably was. He would hold on for three or four miles, and then, if nothing appeared he would give it up. All hands were on deck, hard though it was to stand. The *Matchless* yawed unmercifully with the deck awash.

Crowell argued with himself that he should not go on, should heave to or run under bare poles. Yet ... he would search a little longer. But was he justified? Were the chances he was taking in a whole gale fair to men and ship? He had in his mind's eye the derelict wallowing low in the water, very hard to sight, to the hull to which no man could probably cling. Then he thought of her quite likely gone, sunk.

He was not eight miles at the most from Cape Sable. After a rain squall's truculent passage the clarity behind its blacker cloud extended the visibility to half a mile. And there, suddenly out of the receding squall was an object broad to starboard, a long low-lying hulk. Shouts came from the men as they glanced at the captain who was gazing at the flotsam while at the same time watching the conduct of his vessel. The *Codseeker*!Crowell had almost passed her unnoticed; now she was to windward.

"We'll beat up," he yelled. "Stand to." And to the man at the wheel, "Down helm." It was a long series of tacks to get to weather of what was soon confirmed as the wreck lying on her side, a forlorn sight.

To the amazement of the crew of the *Matchless* they saw figures stretched or huddled face down in the shrouds near the deadeyes. They may have been exhausted or dead. As the *Matchless* came close up on a tack, Crowell put his foghorn to his mouth and blew several blasts. Heads came up gradually and some lifted their shoulders. The *Matchless* men waved and were thankful when they received a feeble response from two who must have had an arm free. That was enough.

Captain Crowell, cautiously elated but with the fear of one who faces unequal odds, saw at close quarters the hazards of rescue. The derelict was awash. His crew would need skill, strength and courage—all that God could give them—to take the poor wretches off. He responded to what he saw with a sailor's compassion, but he was breathing uneasily while he worked his schooner further to

Deadeyes:
Flat circular
blocks of hardwood
grooved around the
circumference and
pierced with three holes;
used in pairs to secure
the ends of the rigging
supporting the lower
masts to the side
of the vessel

windward until she reached a position a quarter of a mile up wind. Hove to, he stood at the taffrail, water running off his oilskin coat, glancing back doubtfully at the eight-oared seine boat at the end of the tow rope. Then he looked down towards the almost hidden wreck. His men were close by; he turned and faced them.

"I don't reckon," he announced in a strong voice above the racket of the storm, "I don't reckon to send anyone over who ain't willing. Who's ready to man the boat?"

Henry Brown, a schooner master in his own right, volunteered at once, knowing he was taking his brother Philip's place. All the others readily followed. Crowell selected the six strongest, the number needed for the boat in addition to Brown. The other two crewmen, Benjamin Newell and Peleg Nickerson, he held back to help him work the schooner and take aboard the survivors.

Manning the boat on the lee side while she leapt and bumped against the vessel was a tricky piece of work. Then it was done; all boarded, the oars unlashed and grasped, and she was pulled clear. They dropped down towards the *Codseeker* with Brown in charge, steering with the long sweep.

The boat came around the stern of the wreck, and at Brown's order, one of the bowmen boated his oar, stood up, balanced himself and threw a line. It fell too far aft for any of the confined men to reach it. He hauled it in, resumed his seat and grasped his oar. They quickly drifted, losing their chance to get in to the quarter where the sea swirled round the stern. As the six men strained at the oars, Brown attempted to steer in amidships. This would bring the boat closer to the marooned men.

Apart from the cataract that periodically surged over the schooner's starboard rail, Brown saw that the seas breaking around the bow turned in and met those coming around the stern creating a turbulence quite unpredictable. The boat, besides contending with the swell, rocked and twisted; but this ceased as the men pulled nearer, and it began to rise and fall in harmony with the schooner, both riding on the same wave.

Brown suddenly saw that his approach, aiming towards a point between the fore and main, was blocked. The sodden foresail barred the way. He might have known she had capsized

Sweep: A long-bladed oar used for steering or sculling a boat or small vessel

while under sail! He altered his tactics and worked towards the bow, avoiding the foretopmast and, with a sign to the rowers, held the boat there while he judged the power against him. Then he urged the boat on a little, steering between the foremast and the bowsprit. They could not board; it was impossible. Being fairly close, the bowman stood up again and heaved a heavier weighted line than he had used before. The wind blew it back. He coiled it and tried again. This time it bent itself around the fore rigging just above three of the stranded men. One took the risk of releasing himself to secure it to the shrouds, with the slowness of a man with numbed hands. It was worth the chance—his only line to life.

Now the boat had a hold on the ship. The oars were taken in, and they warped her by hand towards the vertical half of the pine deck, which stood in front of them. While this manœuvre was full of danger, there seemed no alternative. The connecting rope had to be slackened or taken in skilfully over the bow according to the strain put on the pitching boat; oars could not be used in the encumbered area. They were hauling themselves up close to the bowsprit with the catted anchor on one side and the fore rigging on the other and, more perilous than these, the jib stay beneath them. But they were very close to the wretched survivors. The bowman took a turn around the cleat nearest him. They gestured to the man who was free. He encircled the line with his arms and allowed himself to be washed down to the boat. He was hauled aboard. One more man in the fore-rigging dropped to safety. The third man seemed to hesitate. Yet, in a lull, he finally was persuaded to let himself go and was dragged into the boat.

The two left in the main rigging, bound together, were in greatest jeopardy. Though the distance between the mainmast and the fore was only a few paces, the hazard of traversing the slippery hull was frightening when frequent torrents washed it clean.

The first to leave the rigging made it. The second did not. Letting go, Zebe Hunt started but did not finish. Taken by a wave he simply vanished, for at that moment the boat's bow swung, dipped and caught under the fore shrouds—they had already felt the jib stay lift the boat's after-end. Now it was held down by the

rigging. The sea poured in before the stem was released, but after a perilous moment the mast lifted with the roll of the hulk and the bow came free. The man who made the passage safely swung down the line and was lifted into the flooding boat.

The bowman cast off and four oarsmen got the boat clear, while two bailed and Brown skilfully drifted down over the savage sea to the *Matchless*, which was hove to to leeward, waiting. With much difficulty all hands boarded her. The seine boat was left in tow astern.

A hot fire was burning in the cabin bogey where the four survivors were taken, their clothes pulled off, and their shaking bodies rubbed. When they could eat, they were given food and water. Asked if there could have been any others alive on the *Codseeker*, the answer was "No." It was not possible.

And so the lives of the four fishermen, Jesse Smith, Jeremiah Nickerson, William Goodwin and William Kenney, were preserved, though by a very slim margin. The chance the seine boat took was evident to the crew during their work, yet their concentration on their purpose while amongst the debris of the hulk took the sense of danger partially from their minds.

Thus the master and now six men of the original complement of twelve aboard the *Codseeker* were known to be alive. But it took three days for the news to be heard by their kinfolk ashore. The *Matchless* remained hove to for 50 hours in the storm, which tore the seine boat adrift, before she got under way. She came into Bear Point with her flag at halfmast on May 13 and disembarked her passengers.

TRAPPED BELOW

CHAPTER FOUR

IT WAS NOT AS IMPOSSIBLE AS HENRY BROWN HAD been told that others could have survived that dreadful night and morning. One, Robert Barss, had drowned in the cabin where he had been at the moment of disaster but three men were in the foc's'le. It was to this forward crew-accommodation that James Edwin Smith had gone to get his drink of water. Smith had been knocked senseless when washed off the companionway in his attempt to escape when he realized that the vessel had capsized. He must have recovered quickly for he did not drown while unconscious, and soon his wits enabled him to size up his desperate situation though he was in total darkness.

He found himself up to his neck in water trying to find a footing and at the same time flailing his arms about to keep afloat and to push aside the flotsam attacking his head. He became entangled in blankets, and in his struggle to free himself sheer fright assailed him. With the frantic struggle of a man losing his capacity to breathe he extricated himself. The water was sloshing back and forth, and he moved with it. Suddenly his outstretched hand came in contact with a piece of wood, which this time was firm. He grabbed it. Recognizing it to be the sideboard of a bunk he heaved himself up and clung to its solid support.

He waited, resting. The schooner was obviously sluggish; quite different from the movement Smith knew so well. Now that he had a piece of her structure under his arms he could feel the sodden log-like swaying of a dead ship in a running seaway. Panic almost seized him. He was trapped! No; not yet. He felt around; it was an upper bunk. Pulling his leg on to the board he hauled himself onto it and lay there, clear of the water, wondering, forgetful of his body. He breathed deeply. There was plenty of air here; it was trapped air. The bottom boards of the bunk were gone along with all the bedding, so he had to hold on to the twelve-inch sideboard on which he lay to prevent himself from falling off. Frightening thoughts bore down on him again as his physical preoccupation diminished. How to get out? How could he? If he could not, he would drown!

When would the schooner sink? He knew she was still afloat by her motion. Would anybody come for him? But how could they down here? And no one knew he was in the foc's'le. He was alone. If the air he was breathing became exhausted it would be a horrible way of dying. He was in the bloom of life, only eighteen, he did not want to lose it. The misery of hopelessness had to dissipate; it had to. He must endure and find a way.

More air was in the boat than Smith knew. It had been entrapped throughout the length of the hull in the upper side like a buoyancy tank and kept her afloat. This eventually came to Smith's understanding and gave him some confidence that she was not likely to founder—not yet, at least—and that he would be able to breathe.

But his confidence in the vessel's stability melted when he felt her adopting a ghastly angle in the rising storm. She was going to turn completely over! He clamped his teeth and his heart thumped while she climbed up the precipitous face of a wave, her masts, if they could be seen, pointing steeply downhill. She would be nearly three-quarters over. Smith gripped his slender platform with petrifying urgency, but after frequent repetition without her turning bottom-up, his trust came back slowly and he became used to the motion.

It seemed a long time before he was startled by a new sensation, a trembling in the ship; a shudder, as though the bow had struck something. Then he had a sickening perception of her settling by the head. Water flowed over his body from his feet, which were towards the bow, and then over his face. He sat up grasping the bunk's footboard and pulled himself towards the ship's side above him. There he found air

Foc's'le:
The crew's
accommodation
below decks in
the foremost part
of the vessel,
ahead of the
foremast

again—above the wooden knee tying the deck to the hull, which he felt with his head. The bow continued to sink as though preparing to plunge. Seconds dragged. The inclination remained in spite of her hull being lifted by the waves. She seemed to be tugging like a tethered animal. Smith was holding his breath but not for lack of air. Suddenly the derelict's bow rose. Abruptly the water level, as with a tidal ebb, subsided. Air became more plentiful and Smith slid back to the sideboard, his arms around it and lay face down.

When the schooner had capsized the anchor cable box had slid off the foc's'lehead carrying the chain without the anchor to the shallow bottom. The inner end of the chain had been wired to a ringbolt in the foc's'le deck; thus its full length had been drawn out along the sea-bed as the hulk drifted until it finally caught an obstruction and was held fast. Being waterlogged, her bow responded to the down-ward pull of the cable. Then the wire in the ringbolt broke and she was freed.

Smith dozed off despite the cold water. He dreamed he was on deck with the schooner hove to in a storm. A wave crashed aboard and swept his chum Will Kenney over the side. Though he knew he could not swim, Smith dived after him. He awoke under water snarled in the steps of the companion ladder, which had broken away from its moorings. He extricated himself and floated with the ladder to the bunk board again.

After lying there a long while, during which he tried to avoid picturing himself dying in a saltwater well, he thought he heard a human sound. He listened. Presently it came once more. His eyes tried to penetrate the darkness; his heart thumped again. The sound was a sort of moan or gasp. Smith called out,

"Who's that?" His voice echoed slightly. The reply came, "It's me, Sam."

"Sam?" repeated Smith. "Sam! You there? You all right?" It was Sam Atwood.

"Oh God! That you, Ed? ... Alive?"

Atwood had attached himself in some way to another bunk. Relief filled Smith's mind; he was not alone in that flooded

Admiralty Pattern
Anchor

dungeon. He could face things better with a friend near him. Smith called again but received no reply, and no word came from his further shouts. He thought about it, finally concluding optimistically that he could not be heard over the infernal noise, or more likely, the air pockets were separated by a barrier of water.

Dawn came. Smith could see it was daylight; a glimmer percolated through the companionway some eight feet under water revealing the dreadful shambles in the foc's'le: bits of wood, clothes, bedding, rope, every movable thing in the quarters. He could not see down; the water was misty and the surface frothy. The scene came and went as the trapped water fell when the bow sluggishly pitched down into the trough; rising, it surged up against the side of the vessel overhead, and swirled around him. But he saw Sam Atwood. He was crouching in much the same position as himself, hanging on to the fixed part of a berth further forward. He got sense out of him now. They spoke to one another though they had to do so loudly to be heard even in the lulls. It was good to have a companion. Smith would have reached out and touched him if he were near enough.

They both devoted their thoughts to a method of escape. They talked sporadically about it between the swirling, slopping and splashing of water. The compartment was more than three-quarters full, and its lid, the scuttle to which the ladder had been attached, was too far under water to get at. If they could swim through the hole, fishlike, would they be able to seize anything on an uptilted deck before being washed away? Besides, neither could swim. For the life of them they could not think of a way to get out—and indeed it was their life.

Smith dropped his forehead on the hard wood and cried. Then he cursed his fate and in a passion railed at the builder of the schooner and her owner. They were prisoners without water and food, without hope. There was no means of gaining freedom; they were locked in. The frequent plunging of his body in the cold water forced Smith to direct his mind to his preservation. He felt benumbed.

Companionway: A stairway leading from the deck to a cabin below

Bilge:
The point of
largest circumference
of a barrel, usually
located at the
middle

Night came. The storm had grown worse, evident by the need the men had to cling more strenuously to their tenuous berths. Smith dozed for seconds, woke and dozed again, never quite losing consciousness. His thoughts were sometimes muddled, at others despairing. His home came before his eyes, the meadow, horses, sweet well water to drink ... to drink. He was thirsty.

Light came through the sunken companionway and when Smith looked again—he must have slept awhile—it was much brighter. He felt relatively refreshed. The hulk was fairly still, no longer creaking; the storm had probably blown itself out. He sat up but was taken with wracking pains, and it took a long time to get the cramp out of his legs. He saw that the water beneath him was more or less still.

He and Atwood talked a bit—it was not difficult now because it was much quieter—and the topic soon became fresh water and food. Weak though they were they lowered themselves from their bunks and worked forward to a food locker. On unlatching the door, the contents fell out: two empty bean crocks, a clock and five sodden doughnuts. They devoured the doughnuts in spite of the impregnation of salt tainted with kerosene. Smith then filled the crocks and sank them to get them out of the way.

They rescued the drifting ladder, which supported them both, and in the process of doing so Atwood observed the bilge of a water barrel floating just beneath the surface and, attached to it by a light cord, its wooden pump. Smith grasped the barrel by the chines and raised it just enough to bring the bung clear of the water while Atwood inserted the pump in the bung hole. He put his mouth to the spout and worked the handle. After two gulps he spat; it was brackish.

Smith considered the other food locker but it would be difficult to get at; it was about eighteen inches under water. Nevertheless he peered down. The water was clear now except for debris on the surface, shafts of the sun's rays reflecting up through the water. What he saw he did not expect—the face of a man in a lower bunk on the port side, a face in profile against the ship's side. He nearly let the ladder go. Gazing down, transfixed, he saw that the cook's stove was resting on his legs. It was Will Smith.

The revelation shook them both. Any further search for food was given up; thoughts of death were greater than those of hunger. The idea of going under water was uncomfortable too. They wondered if there were any others drowned down there but Atwood thought not, only two of them had been in the foc's'le when James Edwin Smith had arrived just before the schooner had capsized.

They set about collecting pieces of board and rigged them into staging across their bunks so that they could sleep without falling into the water. They needed the diversion from both the presence of death and the pangs of thirst.

Darkness came again; the familiar foc's'le seemed to turn into a hell hole. They may have slept but it was rather more a state of semi-consciousness in which they groped their way through the night, with dreams and fantasies of escaping through the flooded companionway.

When waking, Smith's thoughts dwelt on dying. What was it like to die from suffocation? No, it would be from thirst. Was the air becoming putrid? Was the water? Smith was tempted to drink the water that surged over him later in the night; the *Codseeker* was tumbling in a rough sea as she had the night before. He could feel her falling off into a pitching motion sometimes and the belching water twisted his clothing and stung his skin. The sea was perishing—that Arctic current always hugging the coast.

Smith found things no longer obscure but what part of the day it was he did not know—dawn? noon? dusk? Atwood had evidently been calling him, but when he did hear him it still took time to understand and answer him. There was a barrel washing back and forth near the lower bunk and Atwood was trying to say that it had biscuits marked on it—'Ship's Hard Biscuits.' Smith immersed himself as soon as he could relieve the pain in his legs, and while Atwood held him he caught the cask. But his hands, particularly his fingers, had so little strength that his grip was feeble, and the thing escaped him. They watched it drifting aft and then it disappeared. On following it they found a jagged opening in the bulkhead separating the foc's'le from the fish hold. It was of course also flooded. They gave up the cask.

Daylight lasted a long time. Smith thought it must have been late in the afternoon when it came to him that the sea had gone down, and the derelict was lying almost still. The two men talked occasionally, mostly not remembering what the other had said. The need for fresh air was on their minds; they seemed to have to breathe more deeply to fill half their lungs.

Lying still on his hard shelf Smith began to experience spasms of shivering, severe at times. He felt colder than usual and wished he could cover himself with any number of dry blankets. During a brief cessation in his more violent fits of ague, he spoke of it in stuttering words to Atwood but received no reply. He thought the rattling boards beneath his shaking body might have told his companion what he could hardly say.

He fell quiet again, exhausted, and drifted off. When he came back to himself he was quite warm, in fact, almost hot. What a luxury! He lay looking into the fading light; all seemed still in the once convivial place where he had mugged-up and eaten good meals and slept with the peace of a simple fisherman. Good meals! He was not hungry any more; he was thirsty. He discovered his clothes were fairly dry outside but wet inside. There was the pain in his limbs, principally in his back, and hot needles were stabbing his muscles. His mouth was thicker than ever and his tongue too big for it.

The night was another one of eternity, silent, mystifying, miserable. He became restless and so hot he wanted to pull off his clothes, which were soaked from fever, but he did not know how to do it. If only he could obtain fresh air and water. He must get into the dark water and cool himself. He tried to call to the Lord as he had done frequently before but could not remember what to say. He thought there must be plenty of fresh water in heaven.

Another day came; it was Sunday though the two men did not know it. They had been confined since the night of

Wednesday. Atwood was awake; Smith could tell that by his heavy breathing and occasional sighing. He could see him too; the sunlight shining through the still water of the submerged hatchway lit the dripping foc's'le. There was almost no movement of the schooner on what was evidently a smooth sea. There appeared to be more headroom in the compartment now that the flood was not swirling about.

Neither man left his platform. Great weakness had overcome them and they were both fever-stricken. Smith was drowsy and had lost track of time. Once he thought he heard external noises, some thumping. It was not Atwood. He gazed absently at a slanting spear of sunlight penetrating the clear water, but he was conscious enough to avoid looking down at the face of the drowned man held fast in his bunk. A clang suddenly startled him—clear, distinct, as though on the hull. He lay motionless. It could not be far away. In the hush came a faint human sound through the wall of the hull ... voices! Muffled voices! Smith shouted, his tortured throat rasping. Atwood yelled. But was it delirium?

OHIO BOARDS A DERELICT

CHAPTER FIVE

THE AMERICAN SCHOONER *OHIO*, CAPTAIN EDWIN DORR sailed from Orland, Maine, on Saturday, May 12, bound for the Grand Banks. On Sunday afternoon, in a light breeze and slightly ruffled sea a few miles west of Seal Island, a black object was sighted abeam at some distance lying low in the water. At first glance it was thought to be a whale and therefore to be disregarded, but keeping his eye on it Captain Dorr noticed that it remained afloat and stationary. Levelling his telescope, he thought it might be a wreck. He altered course.

Soon it was recognized to be a fishing or trading vessel lying on her beam-ends, her tattered jib and foresail lifeless in the water. The *Ohio* bore up close aboard, and the captain made out enough of her name and port of registry from the half-submerged stern to conclude that she was from Barrington. He did not know her. He could see that she was new by the yellowish tinge of her lines and the bright rigging. This was too good to pass up—Captain Dorr could do with some fresh cordage. Being familiar with the laws of the sea, he knew that if he did not choose to tow the wreck in for salvage it was an unwritten privilege to take what he needed from her if she were abandoned.

He sent off six men in two dories equipped with tools to see what they could strip down. They had no difficulty boarding as it was almost calm, and while the older hands were examining the after-end of the vessel two younger fishermen went forward.

Crowell Nickerson's body was not noticed lying silently in the foresail; it must have been covered by a fold in the loosened canvas.

The men clumped about on the side of the hulk in their heavy-soled leather seaboots, and one raised his axe to cut away a high flyer buoy lashed to the fore-shrouds at the sheer pole. With a clumsy swing he came down on the iron strap of one of the deadeyes. It rang out with a clang.

They suddenly heard a muffled voice sounding far away, yet close. After a brief interval there it was again, though they could not catch the word it spoke. Seized with fright, first one, then the other, clambered aft.

"Voice inside!" they hollered to the others in startled wonder. "Voice? Whose voice?"

"Ghosts? It's a ghost!" The two young men were familiar with New England poltergeists and witches. "She's haunted!"

"Don't be stupid," said a middle-aged fisherman, "let's have a look."

They all went forward to the bow and listened. Silence. Then a faint cry. The older man was uncertain himself now. Cupping his hands around his mouth he hailed the *Ohio:*

"Come aboard, Captain. Vessel may have ghosts aboard." Dorr came over in a dory. They told him of the voice.

"What be you talking about—voice?" he demanded. "If them's ghosts below they're live ghosts." He let out a bellow, "Below there!" He got his answer. It sounded like two indistinct words. "Man in the foc's'le!" he exclaimed. "My God!"

He took up the axe lying there and tapped the hull several times at about where he figured the centre of the foc's'le was. They waited in silence. The only sound was the lapping of the wavelets and crying of gulls. At last the response! Two dull knocks

right beneath the feet of one of the men. They had the exact spot. A few more tappings were made to verify the position though from inside only one feeble blow came at a time. But that was enough.

"We'll cut a hole here," Dorr said. He knew there was no other way to enter.

Two men with sharp axes lay into the thick wooden hull. When they tired two others took over so that the axes hardly stopped. With almost the precision of shipwrights, wedges and chips were hewn out as the men moved around their circular task. A blade soon went through and stuck. As it was levered out a gust of air escaped with the noise of a release valve on a steam line. It smelled as though it came from the bilges. They widened the aperture, and the pressure exhausted itself quickly with only a small rise in water level within. The axemen ceased while Dorr crouched down.

"You all right in there?"

"Aye." The one word spoken was weak, husky.

"We'll have you out in a minute. Are you the only one?"

"We're two alive."

Without delay the men resumed their cutting and shaped an elliptical hole about twenty inches across.

"We'll haul you through now," Dorr announced. But the hole seemed hardly wide enough for Smith's broad shoulders and he dropped back. They had no difficulty with Atwood, he was a narrower build. When they held his slight sodden body upright, they saw no colour in his face, and he was taken to be much older than his eighteen years. Two men carefully slid him down into a dory and pulled away.

Time was felt to be pressing so his deliverers attempted again to pull Smith through the opening without waiting to widen it. But it was no use; they had to extend the hole. It took a while. At last they were able to haul him through by his uplifted arms, and though ripping his heavy woollen jersey on the ragged edges of the hole and skinning his ribs, they eased him out into the fresh air. In spite of the pains in his legs and back, half-lying on the now dry warm wood of the hull, joy overwhelmed him. He inhaled the sweet fresh air. He wanted to shout—for a different reason this

Bilge:
The rounded part
of the inside of a vessel's
hull, from the keel to the
point where her sides
rise vertically

time—but he had no throat left to cry out. In his fevered weakness his childhood teaching flashed before him:

"And I saw a new heaven and a new earth." Then he murmured hoarsely, "Sea be beautiful with sun setting to west'ard."

With the last two survivors safely in the cabin of the *Ohio* and the dories hoisted inboard, Captain Dorr made for Barrington Passage, but owing to light winds and calms and strong tides, it was not until eight o'clock the next morning that he reached Shag Harbour.

In the cabin under the quarterdeck Smith and Atwood were bathed and dried, wrapped up and put in bunks with a man to give them a spoonful of water every five minutes. They wanted nothing to eat now, only water; more and more water. "The fire of my thirst was agonizing," Smith said afterwards. The cook made hot potato poultices, which he applied mainly to their extremities. To feel the heat in their feet was comforting.

Captain Dorr himself took Smith to the home of Reuben Stoddart at Bear Point, Smith being Stoddart's adopted son. A letter from Stoddart soon appeared in the Yarmouth Herald praising the crew of the *Ohio* for the rescue and for the great care they took of his son.

Samuel Atwood was accompanied to his home in Barrington by fishermen George Gillpatrick and P. Saunders, and his arrival was greeted with joy, for they had thought him lost, but he still lived. It was four days before James Edwin Smith's thirst was quenched during which time the fever persisted. But this too died away, as did the pain in his feet.

THE OUTCOME

CHAPTER SIX

THERE WAS COMMUNITY REJOICING FOR THE RESCUED and the rescuers and community mourning for the four lost men: Robert Barss, Zebe Hunt, Crowell Nickerson and William Smith. With the rescue of Samuel Atwood and James Edwin Smith, the survivors numbered nine: these two, plus Philip Brown, captain, William H. Goodwin, William E. Kenney, Nathaniel Knowles, Jeremiah Nickerson, Jesse Smith and John Smith.

And the *Codseeker* survived. The schooners *Condor* and *Dove* towed her into Green Cove, Yarmouth County (now Port Maitland) for which they received $450 salvage. Crowell Nickerson's body was cut away from its entangling lines, while the schooner was still lying on her side. She was then righted and pumped out. The body of Will Smith was lifted from his bunk in the foc's'le after the iron stove had been gently removed from his legs. That of Robert Barss was taken from the cabin.

Two months later in July 1877, the *Codseeker* sailed again having been fully repaired, and fisherman James Edwin Smith was back in her foc's'le occupying his old berth. Properly ballasted, she proved to be as seaworthy as any schooner, one of five fishing vessels out of a fleet of thirty-five to make port after the Great Newfoundland Gale of that year.

At least until recently, there was in the possession of his descendants the gold pocket watch presented to Job Crowell by the Honourable Thomas Coffin on behalf of the Government of Canada "in acknowledgement of your humane services in the rescue of four of the shipwrecked crew of the schooner *Codseeker* of Barrington, 9th May, 1877." The nine crew members of the Matchless under Captain Job Crowell each received a $15 reward for "gallant services" and the owner of the *Matchless*, Eleazer Crowell, $30.

The Government of Canada also officially thanked Captain Edwin Dorr of the schooner *Ohio*, for his rescue of two members of the crew of the *Codseeker* "supposed to have perished and restoring them to their friends at considerable pecuniary loss." In a letter addressed to him in Bucksport, Maine, August 16, 1878, he, too, was asked to accept a gold watch "in recognition of your humane services."

SAIL PLAN

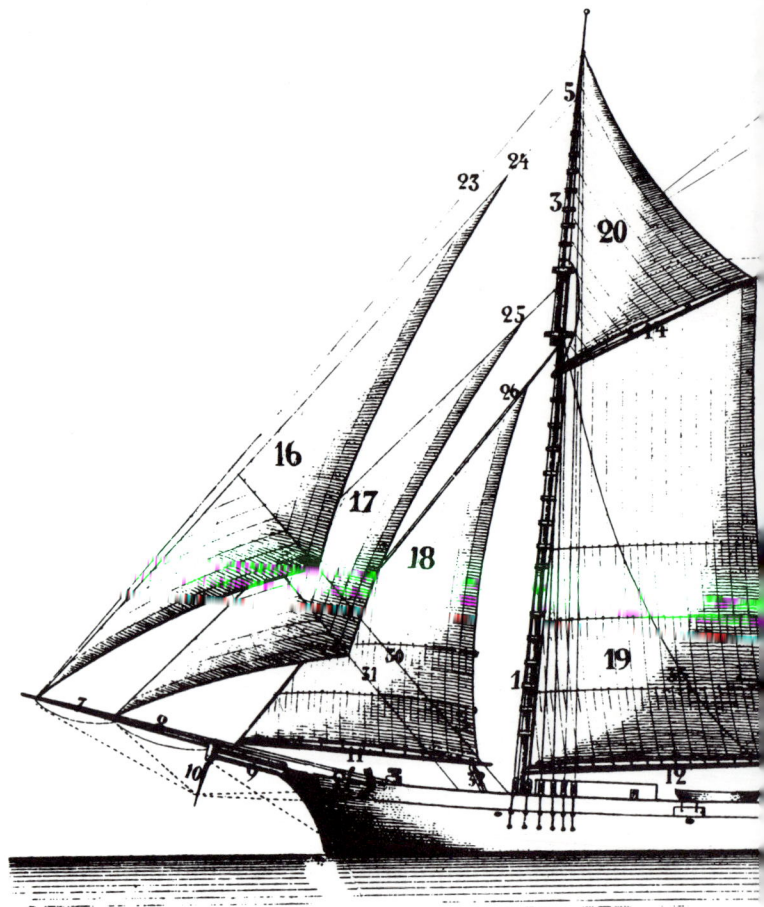

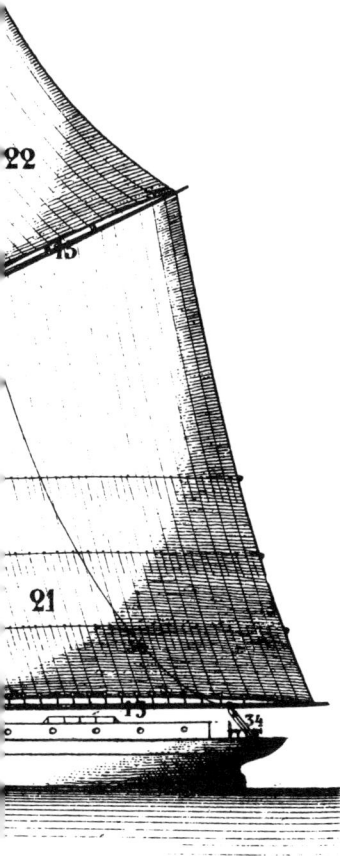

1. Fore-mast
2. Main-mast
3. Fore-topmast
4. Main-top-mast
5. Fore-topgallant-mast
6. Main-topgallant-mast
7. Flying-jib-boom
8. Jib-boom
9. Bowsprit
10. Martingale-boom; Martingale
11. Fore-staysail-boom
12. Fore-boom
13. Main-boom
14. Fore-gaff
15. Main-gaff
16. Flying-jib
17. Jib
18. Fore-staysail; Stay-foresail
19. Fore-sail; Boom-fore-sail
20. Fore-gaff-topsail
21. Main-sail
22. Main-gaff-topsail
23. Fore-topgallant-stay
24. Fore-topmast-stay; flying-jib-stay
25. Jib-stay
26. Fore-stay
27. Main-stay; Triatic-stay
28. Main-topmast-stay
29. Main-topgallant-stay
30. Flying-jib-sheet
31. Jib-sheet
32. Fore-staysail-sheet
33. Fore-sheet; Boom-fore-sail-sheet
34. Main-sheet
35. Fore-topping-lift
36. Main-topping-lift

GLOSSARY

Abeam:
A location or direction at right angles to the fore-and-aft line of a vessel

Aft:
The back end of a vessel

After:
A position further back on a vessel

Beam ends:
Describes a vessel that has rolled so far to one side that her deck is nearly vertical and remains in that position

Beat up:
To sail in the direction from which the wind is coming by a series of alternate tacks or changes in direction across the wind

Bilge:
(Boat) The rounded part of the inside of a vessel's hull, from the keel to the point where her sides rise vertically (Barrel) The point of largest circumference of a barrel, usually located at the middle

Bogey:
A small stove

Broaching to:
The motion of a vessel running before the wind and the sea, whose bow swings around rapidly, increasing the chance of capsizing

Bulwarks:
The portion of the hull planking above the deck that, in rough weather, helps to keep the deck dry and prevent cargo, fittings or crew from being washed overboard

Cabin combing:
The framing or moulding around the base of a vessel's cabin

Careen:
To cause a vessel to heel over

Catted anchor:
An anchor that has been hoisted to the cathead, a heavy piece of timber or iron projecting from each side of the vessel near the bow and fitted with pulleys. The anchor is lifted from the water and supported on the cathead before being stowed away

Companionway:
A stairway leading from
the deck to a cabin below

Davits:
A crane for hoisting and
lowering boats

Deadeyes:
Flat circular blocks of hardwood grooved around the
circumference and pierced
with three holes; used in
pairs to secure the ends of
the rigging supporting the
lower masts to the side of
the vessel

Derelict:
An abandoned vessel

Ditty box:
A small box used by a seaman to hold sailmaking gear
and personal belongings

Down helm:
To turn the wheel toward
the leeward side of the vessel
so the bow will head into
the wind

Falls:
A rope passed through
one or more blocks used
for hoisting

Flotsam:
Cargo or wreckage from a
lost vessel found floating on
the sea

Foc's'le:
(Forecastle) The crew's accommodation below decks in the
foremost part of the vessel,
ahead of the foremast

Foc's'lehead:
The extreme forward end
of the deck

Gale:
A strong wind blowing
at a velocity between 35
and 60 nautical miles an
hour. Within this range of
wind velocities, mariners
distinguish between a
moderate gale, a fresh
gale, a strong gale and
a whole gale.

Gybe:
To swing a fore-and-aft sail
and its boom from one side
of the vessel to the other,
when the vessel is running
before the wind. This may
be done purposely by
altering the vessel's course
slightly, or can happen
accidentally through poor
steering or a sudden wind
shift, endangering the
rigging

Hove to:
To bring the bow of a vessel into the wind and arrange its sails so that it makes no progress and remains more or less stationary. Also, to carry just enough canvas in a storm to keep the vessel facing the oncoming sea

Hulk:
A disabled vessel

Jib stay:
A rope or wire running from the foremasthead to the bow or jib-boom to carry a triangular sail called the jib

Lee shore:
A nearby shore on the lee side of the vessel, i.e., the shore onto which the wind is blowing

Leeward:
The sheltered side, protected from wind and sea

Loom:
The glow in the sky from the hidden beam of a lighthouse

Mast hoop:
A wooden hoop that fits around the mast to hold the foreward edge of a fore-and-aft sail to its mast

Port:
The left side of the vessel, when one is looking forward

Quarter:
The hull of a vessel on either side of the stern

To reef:
To reduce the area of sail spread to the wind by tying up the lower part of the sail

Roadstead:
Protected anchorage for vessels near the shore

Schooner:
(Fishing) A vessel with two masts carrying fore-and-aft sails, the mainsail being much larger than the foresail

Seine boat:
A transom-sterned or double-ended rowboat (approx. 28 feet long) normally used for carrying a long seine net

Sheer pole:
A horizontal rod at the foot of the shrouds, used to spread the ropes above the deadeyes

Shoal:
An off-shore area of shallow water

Shrouds:
Sets of strong ropes extending down from either side of each masthead to the sides of a vessel's hull to support the mast

Sou'wester:
A fisherman's foul-weather rain hat, with a broad brim and a long tail to stop water from dripping down the fisherman's neck. Made from cotton and soaked in a mixture of linseed oil and lampblack

Square-rigged:
A tall ship with two to four masts, carrying square sails on some or all of them

Stand on:
Continue on the same course

Starboard:
The right side of a vessel when one is looking forward

Sweep:
A long broad-bladed oar used for steering or sculling a boat or small vessel

Tackles:
A set of blocks in which rope is used to gain mechanical advantage for pulling or hoisting.

Taffrail:
The rail around a vessel's stern

Thole pins:
The pair of wooden pegs that together serve as an oarlock on a dory or other small boat

Thwart:
The wooden seat in a small boat

Transom:
The flat stern or back end of a dory or larger vessel

Weather:
Toward or lying in the direction from which the wind is blowing; upwind

Wet work:
Work during which the poor sailor gets wet because waves are pouring over the deck of the vessel

Yaw:
To swing wildly off course because a high following sea has thrown the vessel's stern off